I0471448

SPLENDOR

FOR
YOUR

VENDORS

!!!

LITTLE TIPS
FOR

BIG SALES

SPLENDOR
FOR
YOUR
VENDORS!!!
LITTLE TIPS
FOR
BIG SALES

Karen E. Dabney
DABS & COMPANY

SPLENDOR FOR YOUR VENDORS

SPLENDOR FOR YOUR VENDORS!!!
Little Tips for BIG SALES

Copyright © 2013 by Karen E. Dabney

2nd Edition All rights reserved

No part of this manuscript may be reproduced in any form or by any electronic or mechanical means, including information storage and retrieval systems, without permission in writing from the author, except by a reviewer, who may quote brief passages within a review. Any members of educational institutions wishing to photocopy part or all of the work for classroom use, or publishers who would like to include the work in an anthology, should send their inquiries to

Dabs & Company
PO Box 47327
Oak Park, MI 48237-5027, USA

dabsandco@gmail.com

Manufactured in the United States of America

P URPOSE

T HIS handy book will create a more enjoyable experience between hosting organizations, event planners and their vendors no matter how large or small the event.

It will especially appeal to vendors because some of the simplest suggestions inside are often overlooked.

Business owners must keep in mind that vendors are also in business and help lend credence, entertainment, expertise, and excitement to any event. This is because they are also a part of what is bringing people to the events past, present, and in the future!

Even if the event is free of charge to its attendees, it is "selling" something. It may be an idea, a fundraiser, a reception, or information. The impression the attendees leave with will affect how they view an organization for quite some time.

TREATING VENDORS WELL

WILL HELP ALL SELL!

SPLENDOR FOR YOUR VENDORS

Constructive reciprocity is the golden key

to a healthy symbiotic relationship.

~Karen E. Dabney

ACKNOWLEDGMENTS

To those on both sides of the
table,
booth,
partition,
lot,
stage,
store,
hall,
carpet,
doors,
room,
cash register,
window,
loading dock,
microphone,
fence,
stall,
et al …

Your Event!

So, you're having an event and have already put the word out that it's a go. You may have worked with a public relations firm or hired a promoter or both!

You've decided to have vendors present and have alerted your "go tos" — the dependable ones — offering them a discount off the final cost if they register early. On top of that, you are offering a separate discount to any other prospective vendors who register by a certain deadline. You may have even decided to allow the vendors to participate free of charge.
Maybe you are inviting them to advertise in your printed program at a discount.

You've crunched the numbers, mapped the layout, decided on the rules and regulations, have copy for a press release and the contracts, made the initial heads up contact with the media and other connections, and have come to a decision of what the charge(s) – if any – will be for the vendors' participation.

Next you will have:

1. Sent out your press release with the pertinent information, being sure to list those vendors who have already invested in the event and/or are "big draws" as in presenters and products and provided a graphic (attached a photo, flyer, etc.),

2. Decided your overall theme, what types of products to allow and their theme(s), and an appropriate amount of complementary and similar products being offered,

3. Advertised for vendors with the participating cost(s) listed, including a tiered price for the largest to the smallest space per vendor if applicable. Given them information regarding your organization's intentions for the event. Included the name, phone number, and e-mail address for a contact person,

4. Determined how many vendors you can comfortably and legally fit in your venue's sales space and how you will adjust it if you are over or under your limit. Considered those vendors with the need for special accommodations such as a medical issue or demonstration of a product,

5. Prepared the contracts and sent out the acceptance letters along with a flyer in case a vendor wants to self-promote,

6. Received the payments from vendors and/or made payment arrangements; contracts returned and verified, receipts given; returned any moneys paid by vendors who are no longer able to participate. Advertised the vendors and/or their products, using names of either if possible. Most vendors will not have the kind of mass advertising methods or connections that may be at your disposal,

7. Prepared the venue to the best of your ability, exercising whatever power you have to do so.

Prevented favoritism by labelling spaces in a fair and reasonable manner with having at least two people work on the arrangements so they may hold each other accountable.

Be an advocate for your vendors.

And,

8. A day or so before the event – during pre-determined times – assisted vendors with locating their space, transporting them and their wares and equipment, if necessary; making sure they know where to enter and exit and where the restrooms and other amenities are and include those details in an information packets as well as safety and emergency preparedness.

Reassure vendors their property will be as safe as is possible while stored at the venue,

9. Are ready to open the event on time, and

10. Considered the following suggestions on how to create

Splendor for YOUR Vendors!!!

It's YOUR EVENT

but your Vendors:

~appreciate being a part of your event

~represent a business, even if it's a hobby

~know many types of people

~keep your attendees from being bored

~pay with their time and efforts even if their space is free

~make your event more populous

~are able to give directions to restrooms

~are usually generous enough to point an attendee to a product that best meets their needs

~give things away

~have valuable ideas

~are usually thick-skinned

~are pulling for your event to be a success

~are sharing their talents

~will need your help in ways that won't cost
you a cent and won't take much time

~are flexible

~overcome shyness and make connections

~usually know something about your
products and may even have used them

~care about their appearance and
impression

~tell jokes and may entertain children

~are bilingual or more

~have disabilities but still work

~know how to fill their down time

~usually patient

~have unpacking, setting up and packing down to a science

~try to watch another's space if that one has to leave temporarily

~give each other honest criticism

~may not make one sale at your event but know one smile and a card may result in future sales

~may be inviting you to their own big event one day

~usually pick up after themselves

~don't shirk from hard work

~don't "belong" to you

~deserve respect and …

~have "people" knowledge

AND

~do not go "poof" when the event is over!

And Now ...

LITTLE TIPS
FOR
BIG SALES!

THESE tips will increase the probability of your vendors making sales, and will add to the overall excitement and momentum of your event. If you are on a tight budget and unable to follow all of the tips at this time, don't stop reading! These suggestions will stick with you and will become second nature once you are able to implement them. Vendors have many options and want to reach out to as many folk as they can. Most of us prefer a stationary place during a special event. But some like the freedom of being able to roam and sell wherever we can. Some bravely resort to doing "guerrilla" selling and it has advantages: we don't need a table, a backpack or bag full of items will do. We're free to visit the vendors at any event. But we should not approach the attendees unless we are off the event's property and prepared for fallout. Guerrilla tactics are done wherever groups meet. I know folk who go to New York, NY and stand on a street to sell. I like the idea and can see it being successful when I have visited the city. But the open carrying of money on the street, taking it and giving change is kind of a turn off for me, anywhere. But I have done it on many an occasion and always in public; a double edged sword!

The Tips ...

You want to attract and keep vendors of high caliber who will represent your occasion in a positive manner. Following are some ways to help you do just that!

One. When recruiting vendors be upfront and honest regarding what you will provide and what they should expect. Is there a charge for admission? What type of advertising will be/was done? How many attendees are expected? Ask and answer questions as best of you can. Treat their questions as an asset, not a bother.

Two. Be aware that some vendors may experience issues that aren't readily solved, such as an assistant not showing up or equipment problems. Some may have special needs that haven't been met due to their oversight. Although these things are not your responsibility, working with the vendor as much as you are able may help turn things around making both of you look better.

Three. Provide vendors with an attractive and legible ID badge. A show card on their table is a nice touch and may be used to indicate their space if you want to do more than use a number. Include a program for the event. If possible, give them a listing of all vendors, their wares, their booth number, and contact information. Some may be from out of town or not familiar with the area, so give them a listing of nearby eating choices along with the establishments' phone numbers. These gestures of goodwill will benefit you in the short and long run.

Four. It is important to have well-informed, congenial, and patient people at the registration/information desk, not "automatons" or those who behave as if they resent having to be bothered. Some participants — and vendors — at an event will not always have the information on them or may be "directionally challenged." The desk is a good place to get parents' names as well as their children's in case a child gets lost.

Five. Have bottles of cold water available. Invite a company that supplies bottled water and they may supply it free as a product demonstration. Charge a small fee in order to pay for someone else distributing the water if necessary. However, it is thoughtful and classy to have free bottled water — and more — for your vendors. Poll them ahead of the event to determine their interest in how the possibility of a provided meal could be handled.

Six. Use "floaters" allowing a vendor a quick break if they are at a table by themselves. While the vendor is gone, a sign may be placed stating they will return soon and the floater can try to remain in the general area, perhaps enlisting the assistance of vendors nearby.

Seven. Do not forget your vendors. Announce the fact before and after breakfast, brunch, lunch or dinner that there are vendors to visit and mention a few of the types of items available. An exception may be if the event is a fundraiser and the vendors are working with a participating organization or donating a portion of their sales toward the fundraiser. Another exception may be if your event is mainly focused on selling a particular product. If the vendors are directly related to a particular cause or service, announce that at steady intervals; perhaps more than three times at a large event and at least twice at a small one. Help the vendors out by mentioning their product because you will already have the attention of the crowd. Be upbeat about it. This should not be the vendor's job. If convenient, invite them to speak but don't leave it to them to approach the emcee and possibly be rebuffed. If a vendor doesn't wish to address a group, don't put them on the spot. Just say a few words about them and let them wave from their seat. I am not always willing to speak even though I usually do an excellent job. If the vendors' product relates directly to a particular segment of the event, be sure to incorporate them into the activity.

I was one of several children's book authors in an intimate setting during a conference where other activities were taking place. The event's literacy component (a subject I am extremely concerned with and trying to encourage through my books) took place in one room and we were all lined up at tables in the back of it. People were speaking about how to get youth to read and not once were we vendors publicly acknowledged. We had become a part of the whole, not highlighted when the moment was ripe. A lot of attendees need to be invited or reminded of and guided to what is available to them!

E*ight.* If your event involves youth of any age, include an area for children to expend energy. Ideally, it should be in proximity of some vendors whose products relate toward families, education, sports, and the like. Provide an activity such as scrap art, face painting, a demonstration of products for youth, and such. If you are using a character (such as a clown) of any kind, arrange for the character to be a "pied piper" to lead the children around to view the wares that may be of interest them. Give the children cards to get stamped by each vendor they visit. If they get a certain number of stamps, they can be entered into a drawing and can also show their parent what items they wish to have (Make sure they will be led back to where they started from. It may prove necessary.). This method can also be used effectively with adults. A mascot/celebrity may be more expensive but it all depends on what you are aiming for and can afford. A less expensive way would be to announce there are cards/tickets available for those who wish to participate in a drawing at each table. The vendor will label and give the ones with participants' names to a member of your organization. Hold a few drawings during the event. If possible and appropriate, announce the winners. Doing so will cue the participants to return to the vendor to claim their prize. Others will follow to see this happen. If you have the media present this will certainly be considered a photo opportunity!

N*ine.* Most large events are formed around one theme. However, some items are appropriate at any gathering — as well as some that may not be. Know your audience and the difference. It may be possible to find a common denominator to justify any grouping.

Ten. Let the vendors know if there is a preferred way for them to dress and if they need to make special accommodations for any of the participants. For example: is this a "family friendly" event? Is the gathering for a special group such as the visually impaired?

Eleven. If your vendor area has a lot of bare wall space and is not the type of place where banners, etc., can be hung, use the space for subtle, unobtrusive posters or signage. Be careful with overuse of signage lest your venue take on the look of a sports arena's wall or a race car driver's jumpsuit unless those are components of the business you're promoting.

A well-thought out event I participated in had a lot of bare walls. This was at a college during a well-attended cultural event. I suggested for next year the coordinator solicit artwork from the college's students and/or various schools and hang it. I feel it more appropriate of an attraction when the youth are featured. The work could be exhibited for sale as well as decoration

(Inform the buyers they would not be able to receive the artwork until after the event.). Doing so would also encourage attendees to visit all of the vendors. This type of thing is especially necessary for those vendors who find themselves in the back corridors away from the entertainment. In such a situation the pied piper idea above would help greatly.

T*welve.* Here's an excellent form of in-kind cooperation! I was recently at a major event where others and I who had items pertaining to youth were allowed to have free tables and set up in a special area for children. We were welcome to perform and provide an activity or just interact with the children. The children were safe, entertained, and able to do what children do. The only thing I feel was missing was a mascot type character and some folk working as roaming security — possibly disguised as characters — to keep an eye on the youth as we vendors cannot sell and do both. I believe parents/guardians would have felt more comfortable allowing their children free rein in the area had they known there were people whose main duty was to watch over them.

Again, collect names and cellular phone numbers (even if already done at a registration booth) if feasible. The information should be returned to the parent/guardian (you may want to check ID) when they come to pick up their child. I suggest you have them come at least 1 hour before the event ends. The children remaining later MUST have a responsible adult in the same area. Remind the parents/guardians not to abuse the courtesy. Decide if you should charge a fee if providing child care and have the necessary qualifications to operate such. Let the parents know if there is an end time. Provide them with a number to call in case of an emergency.

T*hirteen.* Keep a list of vendors − past and present − handy so you can refer them to your customers during the event and in the future. You may want to collect multiple business cards from each vendor, and stamp your information on the back (or attach a label) as the referrer. This works both ways!

F*ourteen.* Any time you have planned an event, accept business cards/small flyers from the vendor/entertainer a few weeks before and put them in a bag your customers may use for purchases or as things to put in a "swag bag" making it fuller and more useful. This almost guarantees a more than cursory look later. Do not rely on the customer to pick these items up from a counter or table. Also, I see many folk take flyers, cards, etc. from a person handing them out, then toss them away. Some seem to take the information out of politeness. Do not count on handing folk advertising information alone. Adding the ability to use it as a coupon may increase the likelihood the receiver may hold onto it. It would help to have the words "FREE", "COUPON", and "SPECIAL" to catch the receivers' attention.

F*ifteen.* The titles vendor and entertainer sometimes meet. Rarely is a person who is basically seen as a vendor be paid for presenting at an event. Sometimes a deal may be made where the price of the selling space is reduced or some other perk. But the person does not enjoy most of the benefits unless they are well-known and/or considered an expert in the industry. You may see a celebrity at a booth in order to attract buyers but they will not be doing the physical work or remaining at the sales spot for long. And they will probably have all of their expenses covered by the host AND receive a fee. They are some of the happiest looking, hard working folk you will see at any event. But so, too, are the ones who are seen as vendors only. Many vendors do extremely well because they have a following and are more accessible to their fans for a much longer period of time. They usually don't have to rush and their followers will wait because they are not rushing either. And because the quality and popularity of the vendors' wares often speak for them, they don't have to talk as much as the celebrities. They are some of the most serene, hard working folk you will see. Some are part of a group and they bring others with them who are the "draw" and allow those to circulate while they remain friendly and stationary.

Hint: Most successful vendors have more than a bit of an actor in them, even the quiet ones.

So, you will need to be flexible when you have a featured special guest/vendor or a vendor with a special product. There are some things you should do for either. If you book someone at your venue, remember to put the information on your website even if it is at the last moment. Some will see it and tell others. Better done early than late but better late than not!

Let your scheduled guest know if you are unable to guarantee making flyers so he may have a chance to deliver his own. Most will not need to be told but once the event is a sure thing (a "sure thing" to me means written), let them know — just in case — they should put out their own information. Your organization is also responsible for spreading the word. Remember: the vendor/entertainer is a temporary member of it. If you have staff doing press releases, have a mass mailing list, and can otherwise help broadcast the event, you should do so. This should be second nature as you both have the same overall objective. Possibly, your event is being treated as a joint effort; then refreshments, etc., should be handled jointly unless the guest is a celebrity, was invited by you, and will be paid for their appearance. Then you are responsible for all of the expenses related to having that person present.

Do not look at promoting the "typical" or lesser known vendor as something they should have to pay for unless they are buying personal advertising space in your program book, website, etc. They, too, are part of the draw to your venue. Where would Facebook be without its members who pay nothing to meet on the site?

A small thing such as a listing of the vendors and their products to hand out is enough to help them be sought out.

S*ixteen*. Some venues (mary reluctantly
agree to) provide basic refreshments when
they have a guest who is selling their own
product, and usually expect a percentage of
products sold. What is wrong with this
picture is the vendor — who is not being
paid otherwise — should not be the only one
providing refreshments. The worst case
scenario — within reason — is either the
vendor — or your venue — having no sales
and a poor showing. This is not fun for
either of you and may be more than a bit
embarrassing especially for a lone vendor!
But if the vendor had to pay for
refreshments, transportation, and getting
their merchandise to your venue, they have
lost much more than just their time. They
most likely are not renting out your entire
space. They aren't preventing you from
selling your merchandise. They are hoping to
attract buyers so you both may benefit. And
usually, they are not taking up much time or
space or causing you to oper much earlier or
close much later. You would have been
there with the lights on anyway unless you

changed your hours for the event. If the vendor is renting your venue, they have the right to your directing attendees toward them and removing items that are similar to what they are offering (If you are not present, they are in charge, so don't give this power to someone you do not know well unless you provide your own manager and/or security.).

Be fair with the vendors. Place a flyer advertising their date in your customers' hand to assist with publicity. Include them in your budget. Encourage your clientele to come. Even if it is just to mosey around for a while, it will help. People are drawn to where there are others. They look for parking spaces already filled, folk milling about inside and outside. Your regular customers may bring another with them. They may actually like what they see and purchase something. That becomes infectious to the others in your venue. They may not buy today, but they will usually accept a card or coupon with the vendor's information and a sale may result in the future. Allow the vendor to use their own sales method listed on their card/coupon unless you have already agreed to place their product in stock. You may see the value of it even if the event was not profitable. If sales for the vendor go poorly, you have basically lost only the price of refreshments. Sometimes this happens no matter how hard the person has worked in their preparation. It may take a while to build up sales but if you keep having special events, your "regulars" may begin asking what the next one will be!

S*eventeen*. Be supportive of vendors and allow a return visit when you can. As long as they respect your space and aren't out of place, they are still a special event and add variety to your venue.

E*ighteen*. Important: If you have a headliner, do what is done at music performances — let the lesser known person go first — if appropriate, or acknowledge them on the flyers, etc. you will provide before the event and on a program you will be giving out at the event, if possible. Give them signage or allow them to provide and place it before the event. I have participated in events where the headliner went first and I was basically overlooked before and after. At one of them, mine was a last minute invitation. There were no flyers listing me and what I'd be doing. The reason I was there did not get mentioned before or immediately after the other person's part. A few folk stopped by my table but most had risen as one and left as soon as the headliner did. It may have helped keep folk there and for them to notice me if the headliner had done a question and answer period before leaving. Or, my product could have been quickly mentioned as soon as the headliner was about to leave. Something like: "For those of you who have a young person at home who likes to read, we have author Karen E. Dabney available with her books." Another time, I was suddenly asked to fill-in for an extremely famous children's author. When I arrived, I saw signs stating the author would not be appearing without any mention of a substitute. Needless to say, I soon saw a lot of classes being turned around by their teachers before entering the building because a sign was posted on the outside doors that the other author had to cancel. I was a bit rattled but able to speak to an openly disappointed group.

Why the person who invited me didn't stop the staff from placing the signs without listing a substitute was coming was beyond me. She also made no effort to gather any of the classes as they were leaving. I had to encourage the group who remained to give me a chance. Fortunately — for my ego and time — a father and daughter who were not part of the group happened to be listening to my reading. The daughter wanted a book and I left feeling somewhat appreciated and less used. But I always appreciate the opportunity. The people inviting me meant well and there may have been more sales to be made. So as long as I wasn't otherwise occupied and it would not cost me a lot of effort and travel, I am usually happy to attend. I loved speaking with the children, anyway!

This is a something to be cognizant of: when you invite an author – or any other visitor to do anything – both of you should be clear regarding if the visitor will be paid, products purchased and/or allowed to be sold. Sometimes I do visits for no cost to an organization and expect nothing but a good experience. However, I am not in the position – yet! – of being able to do so frequently. So, when I go to a place and not one book or other item is purchased, that tells me something about the people responsible for my coming. And, when I bring up the question beforehand, many will say something like, "We "just" want you to come read to the children." So, I seem selfish and mean when I politely say I can't do the appearance.

Please look up what an author usually charges to "just" read to a group.

N*ineteen.* For a one-time event appearance on a small scale where money is involved, you may feel it fine to basically go by each other's word. I — personally — want to have the agreement in writing and would advise all events be handled that way. A simple form listing who does what would suffice, including a consignment agreement if you will be selling the vendor's products in your store. However, for a large undertaking and/or recurring event — such as a class or performance — a written agreement is definitely in order. It is not professional or fair to expect either party to agree to do something of the kind without it being put on paper. If the event fails to take place, it is usually the performer's reputation that will be questioned. And — of course — they will want to defend themselves when approached by those who want to know what happened.

Be aware that when it comes to reputation, you want to keep a positive one as far as vendors/ entertainers are concerned
Talk travels too!

T*wenty.* Consignment is another issue that can put the vendor at a serious disadvantage.

To be honest, I look forward to the day when I don't need to do it! The additional roles of, supplier, accountant, ballet dancer, spy, collector, enforcer, and lawyer can quickly become a vendor's nightmare if they don't have someone to handle those issues. The vendor is happy to have their work selected and placed in a store. The usual sixty/forty split is not bad considering the host is willing to share their customers and space with vendors and getting an agreement on paper is usually not a problem. But … rarely do stores give an accounting of their consigned sales, so the vendor has to gingerly inquire about their own item(s) so as not to be a pushover or a pest. There have been times where people I know have purchased my products and tried to find out how many of my items remained available. Sometimes they could, most times they couldn't. And they usually let me know if, when, and from where they have purchased my work. One store had sold all seven of the books I had there but when I called and was told there was one left (Consignment would renew after all of the first agreement were sold.). When I was told by the six friends who bought one each, I realized the manager was treating the review copy as one of the inventory. This was my fault because I had forgotten to write the words "review copy" on it. When I gave the manager the names of those who had purchased the books, we were able to get things straightened out. The remaining book no longer prevented me from being able to renew and she graciously took more than the first set because they were selling. Now, with some places, even if I found out they were out of stock it didn't make collecting my share of the money much easier.

I understand that sometimes it takes a while to "cut a check" but more than a month without any communication? C'mon, now! And I don't like telling someone my books are at a place where they can't be found! Here's the kicker: Keep good track of your items if they are for sale on consignment. Read the agreement. Some stipulate that any items not sold or picked up by a certain date automatically belong to the store. Vendor Be Aware!

Twenty One. I have had to remove my items from several stores due to varying issues. I even had to bring up small claims court to get less than $80 that was owed to me for over two years! Another took months to pay me less than $10! And another "store" — due to my naiveté — outright stole an amount of books that I have never recouped. A producer of the Judge Judy courtroom show invited us to Hollywood to appear and settle the matter but the absconder was too smart to do that one. I thought she'd want to come because everything would be paid for and she could bring fake witnesses (Now you know why they usually are painfully, obviously ignorant of the details of the situations when called upon.) on a trip to Hollywood. When she resurfaced and answered my latest e-mail request to settle, she accused me of just wanting to promote my books. Um, yeah. That and get my money or books back (in excellent condition, of course). So, you see, even the inconvenience of going to court does not guarantee the vendor will get his money or even that the defendant appears. Some folk have radar when it comes to avoiding a process server. However, the record of his claim will be noted and available if a search is performed on the company or individual. Trusting the untrustworthy is a sure-fire way to learn and shed some green (double entendre intended). But vendors, don't just suck it up. One complaint may help bring forth others. The dollars that have to be chased or let go add up folks! Therefore, it is especially pleasing for a vendor to do business with those who can — and do — pay upfront for placement or directly after a sale from an event.

Twenty Two. Be sensitive to how your behavior may affect the vendors. I was taken aback at one event where I was selling my books and during the whole time, there was a group giving away books for free that rivaled my and other participating vendors' books! None of us sold much that day. And we were already riding the coattails of a celebrated author with the fans dwindling away as soon as he stopped signing books. Not cool but not intentional, either. I think they could have given out the other books as an incentive to get folk to purchase from the vendors. There were many, many books so each book purchased could have meant as much as two free books per book purchased. And there could have been drawings throughout the event for a free book to help keep attendance up. After the end of our event, children could have been invited to take a book from the free collection; some of which could have been held back and brought out for those who may not have gotten one earlier. Now, don't get me wrong. I always provide some type of free activity or gift from my table. I know a lot of kids wouldn't have gotten a book were there not some available for free. I may even be the inventor of a free "Signature Sheet" for authors: Whenever I hold an event with

other authors, I design a sheet listing their names and their book title cn it. I leave enough space for each author to sign so every child may leave with the autograph of all of us "real authors" they met that day. Perfect for "Show and Tell".
(I wrote the above critique regarding the free books as a straight business matter.)
However, I can't gripe too much. We were allowed to participate for free at a large, annual, family friendly event.

Twenty Three. Some organizations are very diplomatic regarding vendors leaving early and an empty space in their wake. I am one of those wait-until-the-last-minute sellers. If an event is being advertised as from 1 PM until 4 PM, breaking down should not have to begin until after 4 PM. I want my half-hour — especially if I paid for it! As most of us know, many customers wait until the near end before they make their buying decisions. Still, I have been aggressively rushed to break down before the actual ending of some events. This bothers me because I have a piece of paper that says one thing but I am usually expected to do another. And, this is the norm. It is wrong of both parties but is a "Which came first; the chicken or the egg?" type of thing. I feel it is partly due to the practice of most vendors breaking down a half an hour before the end time or earlier. Some may even leave after the first hour if things are slow. These are usually the vendors who have not been featured in some way and may not be well known. And, sometimes they are the ones who don't have much patience if things weren't well-planned, no matter their stature. If there is a low turn-out or no one is paying, they leave and take their "ball" with them. This is not fair to the host but I've noticed few complain. I think that may be because they have become resigned to it or their agreement with the owner(s) of the venue meant they expected all to have left by the end time. And that is tantamount to misleading the vendors which can be interpreted as a lack of concern, and the cycle continues. Understandably, it has become more common for those in charge of the event to insist vendors remain for the duration. Perhaps an incentive could be offered before the crucial half-hour to delay vendors departing? I know, it shouldn't be necessary but it may stop some of the "tit for tat" behavior as mentioned above. After all, you may be losing money as the "ghost" space is not in keeping with the image you want to present (Perhaps you could hurry and place a cloth and some items on a table or in an empty space.). Myself, I would not want my attendees/customers to have to pick their way through dismantled displays, furniture and boxes. I would have vendors wait until all attendees were expected to have left the event — at the end time listed for the vendors. Also, I want to be available to those I have let know when I expect to be leaving. It is easy to blame the host or the vendors if things go wrong. Who blames whom depends on how the event went for either. Key questions: How thoroughly was the event planned and heavily was it promoted?

Twenty Four. The completion of anonymous evaluation forms from vendors is becoming a thing of the past. In my opinion, it should be continued because it is an extremely important part of communicating our honest feelings and having them taken into consideration. E-mail does not necessarily provide anonymity due to "Captcha" and other devices.

Twenty Five. Another issue that is not the responsibility of the venue is the safety of the vendors — especially women. We are at an event seen taking in money and may be leaving the event alone in the dark. It would be greatly appreciated if anyone available would watch/walk us to our cars, whenever possible. Another method would be a pick-up point for which vendors would be given a number, get their cars in that order and be able to load up at a door(s) A valet service could be used instead but still respecting the number *order*. I also feel any additional, thoughtful service generates goodwill and should be considered a part of what is available to all vendors, even if for a fee. This would be another way to encourage everyone to leave at the same time. Sort've like the end of a movie: Those of us who like to read the credits are usually in good company!

So, now you've read my little tips. I hope they have been helpful. Now add your own before you get "re-busy" and forget about them!

SPLENDOR FOR YOUR VENDORS

SPLENDOR FOR YOUR VENDORS

_____

_____

_____

_____

_____

_____

_____

_____

_____

_____

_____

_____

_____

_____

_____

_____

_____

_____

_____

_____

_____

_____

_____

SPENDID!

SOME PRAISE!

I have been in many venues — as part of a group and an individual — where I felt especially valued and pleased whether I had sales or not. The ambiance and behavior of my hosts made all the difference. I always view any event as a chance to be seen and relate to the public as promotion. I make it a point to be pleasant and look the part even it seems I may be leaving with exactly the same amount of my items I arrived with. Those who are angry and allow their faces to sour are ending their day in a negative way that will affect all concerned. This further stresses the importance of the opportunity to express opinions and share suggestions on an anonymous evaluation form. Disappointments written out may reveal areas where improvement can be made and allow for vendor venting (smile). I also think it would be helpful if a representative of the event – big or small – made it a point to visit and thank each vendor and trade business cards with them sometime during the event. And — of course — that is another "works both ways" type of thing. Most of us don't think to send a thank you note to a large organization. However, someone will read and appreciate it. I just finished writing a card to thank the person at one of the latest events in which I was included. Going to remember to do so more in the future too!

A BIG THANK YOU to the hosts who have treated me extra-well in my efforts to sell!

~Karen

AFTERWORD

THERE is no way to guarantee sales will be made for all vendors and that all the promotion in the world will work to bring in a large crowd. But as long as we all work toward our goals, that probability increases things turning out in everyone's favor (maybe even if there is an unexpected snow storm). Sometimes a venue can improve the odds by creating a similar event and encouraging past vendors to return every year. The attendees will learn they can find their favorite, yet obscure, quilt maker there. And the vendors may plan their schedules to participate even before being approached. It helps to allow a vendor to visit a venue more than once to garner attention or, to be known for a special theme.

Six of the most successful events I've had were where I shared my books and expertise with (1.) a large agency on how to write for children, (2.) spoke about literacy: the necessary ingredients for getting youth to read, (3.) reminding parents of their power and part at a parents' organization meeting, (4.) speaking briefly in a school staff meeting, (5.) teaching a summer program where a total of 18 books of mine were purchased for it, and (6.) selling during a school holiday festival which led to one of the administrators arranging to meet me between two scheduled events and purchasing six additional books as Christmas gifts. I have also had great success being invited to work with experts in the field during conferences or lectures.

As those in charge and those at-large we must all respect what each other has to offer, work together developing and keeping each others' best interest at heart, and own our parts in ensuring a great experience no matter what. In the bigger picture, are we not ALL service providers (vendors)?

Positive Symbiotic Relationships Nourished
Will Cause All Sales To Flourish!

WORK TOGETHER SELL TOGETHER SHINE TOGETHER!

SPLENDOR FOR YOUR VENDORS

About the Author

Karen E. Dabney, a native Detroiter, possesses a BFA from The University of Michigan and a BA from the University of Detroit Mercy, and a natural-born salesperson!

Karen attended writing workshops with the Voices of Our Nation's Arts Foundation (VONA) and The Hurston/Wright Foundation. She is a member of the International Reading Association, National Association of Teachers of English, National Conference of Artists, The Southern Poverty Law Center, Motown Writers' Network, Broadside Poets' Theatre, Concept East, Project B.A.I.T., Urban Theater Magazine, Women Who Write, Gifted in Michigan, Detroit Unity Poets' and Authors' Society (DUPAAS), and ART4EYES&EARS!

Karen is the owner of Dabs & Company; an organization dedicated to promoting literacy and keeping minds 'lit'.

Books by
Karen E. Dabney

~*The Magic Pencil*
~*The Magic Pencil Black Language Glossary*
~*The Magic Pencil Curriculum Guide*
~*I am a YoungStar and I Love Me Some ME!*
~*I am a YoungerStar and
I Love Me Some ME Too!*
~*StarLeader Guidebook*
~*Jenga*
~*Unhappiness Is ...*

Books by

Dabs & Company
~*Necessary Roughness by Safi*
~*The Elephantom in the Room by Nuru*
~*Dreaming by Chicara J. Brassell*

SPLENDOR FOR YOUR VENDORS

Dabs & Company
PO Box 47327
Oak Park, MI 48237-5027
313.632.3384/313.451.2628
dabsandco@gmail.com
www.dabs-and-company.com

WORK TOGETHER SELL TOGETHER SHINE TOGETHER!

SPLENDOR FOR YOUR VENDORS

SPLENDOR FOR YOUR VENDORS

SPLENDOR FOR YOUR VENDORS

www.ingramcontent.com/pod-product-compliance
Lightning Source LLC
Chambersburg PA
CBHW051222170526
45166CB00005B/2006